Kevin Garnett

by Arlene Bourgeois Molzahn

Reading Consultant:
Dr. Robert Miller
Professor of Special Education
Minnesota State University, Mankato

CAPSTONE
HIGH-INTEREST
BOOKS

an imprint of Capstone Press
Mankato, Minnesota

Capstone High-Interest Books are published by Capstone Press
151 Good Counsel Drive, P.O. Box 669, Mankato, Minnesota 56002
http://www.capstone-press.com

Library of Congress Cataloging-in-Publication Data
Molzahn, Arlene Bourgeois.
    Kevin Garnett/by Arlene Bourgeois Molzahn.
    p. cm.—(Sports heroes)
    Includes bibliographical references and index.
    ISBN 0-7368-0778-0
    1. Garnett, Kevin, 1976—Juvenile literature. 2. Basketball players—United
States—Juvenile literature. [1. Garnett, Kevin, 1976– 2. Basketball players.
3. Afro-Americans—Biography.] I. Title. II. Sports heroes (Mankato, Minn.)
GV884.G37 M65 2001
796.323'092—dc21   00-010091

Summary: Traces the personal life and basketball career of the Minnesota
Timberwolves' forward.

Editorial Credits
Matt Doeden, editor; Lois Wallentine, product planning editor; Timothy Halldin,
    cover designer and illustrator; Katy Kudela, photo researcher

Photo Credits
Allsport USA/Nathaniel C. Butler/NBA, cover; Todd Rosenberg, 18, 21; Brian Bahr,
    23; Ronald C. Mondra/NBA, 28; Harry How, 32, 35
AP Photo/Tony Gutierrez, 7
Reuters/Eric Miller/Archive Photos, 4
Reuters/Sam Mircovich/Archive Photos, 16
SportsChrome-USA, 10, 24, 42; Brian Spurlock, 9, 13, 27, 31, 41; Michael Zito, 14,
    36, 38

3 4 5 6 06 05 04 03 02

Table of Contents

Chapter 1   Team USA 5

Chapter 2   The Early Years 11

Chapter 3   A Big Jump 19

Chapter 4   The NBA 25

Chapter 5   Kevin Garnett Today 37

Features

NBA Per-Game Statistics 9

A Hero's Hero.. 16

Career Highlights 43

Words to Know 44

To Learn More 45

Useful Addresses 46

Internet Sites 47

Index 48

Team USA

It was July 25, 1999, in the city of San Juan, Puerto Rico. Kevin Garnett was playing in the Olympic Qualifying Tournament with the United States' basketball team. The top two teams in the tournament would qualify for the 2000 Olympic Games in Sydney, Australia.

Team USA began the tournament with a game against Uruguay. Kevin and his teammates were among the best players in the world. They were also among the tallest. Kevin stands about 7 feet (2.1 meters) tall. He and his teammates towered over Uruguay's shorter players.

Kevin played in the Olympic Qualifying Tournament in 1999.

Team USA jumped out to an early 10-2 lead. Minutes later, the score was 24-8. Kevin and his teammates did not let up. At one point, they led by 53 points.

Kevin was the star of the game. In the second half, he scored 8 points within 90 seconds. He also scored one of the game's most exciting baskets late in the second half. Guard Gary Payton had the ball. Payton passed the ball through his legs to Kevin. Kevin caught the pass and dunked the ball. The basket gave Team USA a 99-46 lead. Moments later, the two players left the floor. The crowd stood and cheered. Kevin scored 20 points during the game. The final score was 118-72.

Kevin's great play continued throughout the tournament. Early in the tournament, many of the fans would not cheer for Team USA. They thought it was unfair that the team was so much better than the other teams. But more and more fans cheered for Team USA as the tournament went on. Kevin's play and personality were two of the biggest reasons. The fans enjoyed Kevin's powerful dunks. They also liked his wide smile.

Kevin led Team USA to the tournament championship.

> My approach to the game of basketball from day one is passion, emotion, and fun. I want to have fun and win.
> —Kevin Garnett, Press Conference, 7/25/99

Kevin played in all 10 of Team USA's games. He scored a total of 119 points and had 70 rebounds. Team USA easily won all 10 games and the championship. Kevin and his teammates had assured Team USA of a place in the 2000 Olympics.

About Kevin Garnett

Kevin Garnett plays both small forward and power forward for the Minnesota Timberwolves. He is one of the best and most popular players in the National Basketball Association (NBA). During the 1999–2000 season, Kevin made the All-NBA team and the All-NBA defensive team. He also finished second to Los Angeles Lakers' center Shaquille O'Neal in the Most Valuable Player (MVP) voting.

Kevin is successful off the court as well. In 1997, he became the highest paid athlete in team sports. He signed a contract for $126 million. Kevin also endorses products such as Nike shoes. He earns millions of dollars each year for appearing in these advertisements.

CAREER STATISTICS

Kevin Garnett

NBA Per-Game Statistics

Year	Team	Games	Points	Rebounds	Blocks	Assists
95-96	MIN	80	10.4	6.3	1.64	1.8
96-97	MIN	77	17.0	8.0	2.12	3.1
97-98	MIN	82	18.5	9.6	1.83	4.2
98-99	MIN	47	20.8	10.4	1.77	4.3
99-00	MIN	81	22.9	11.8	1.55	5.0
00-01	MIN	81	22.0	11.4	1.79	5.0
Career		448	18.5	9.5	1.78	3.9

CHAPTER 2

The Early Years

Kevin Garnett was born May 19, 1976, in Greenville, South Carolina. His mother is Shirley Garnett. His father is O'Lewis McCullough. Kevin's parents never married. He lived with his mother and his older sister, Sonya.

Shirley married Ernest Irby when Kevin was 7. The family moved to Mauldin, South Carolina, when Kevin was 12 years old. By this time, Kevin also had a younger sister named Ashley.

Kevin Garnett was born May 19, 1976.

A Talented Player

Kevin wanted to be an athlete at an early age. He wanted to play football. But his friends convinced him to play basketball instead. Soon, Kevin discovered that he was better at basketball than his friends. He then decided that he wanted to be a professional basketball player.

Kevin's stepfather did not want him to play basketball all the time. Kevin wanted to put a basketball hoop in the family's driveway. But Ernest would not let Kevin have one. Instead, Kevin played basketball at Springfield Park near his home.

Kevin played basketball whenever he could. He practiced shooting, dribbling, passing, rebounding, and blocking shots. He wanted to be a complete player. Kevin enjoyed playing against his friends. But he practiced alone when his friends grew tired of playing.

Kevin's life included more than basketball. He often had to care for Ashley while their mother was at work. Shirley did not want him

Kevin learned at an early age that he was a talented basketball player.

to play basketball all the time. She hoped that Kevin would study hard in high school. She wanted him to go to college. She hoped that he would become a social worker.

Learning The Game

Kevin played for Mauldin High School's basketball team when he was in ninth grade. James Fisher was Kevin's coach. He told Kevin

Kevin still wears a rubber band around one ankle or wrist while he plays.

that there was more to basketball than just scoring. He coached Kevin to become a team player. He taught Kevin to pass the ball to his teammates. Kevin averaged 12.5 points and 14 rebounds per game during that season. Kevin also was a great defensive player. He averaged seven blocks per game.

Kevin put a rubber band around his ankle or his wrist before he started each game. He hoped the rubber band would bring him good luck. He sometimes snapped the rubber band to remind himself to work hard.

Kevin became friends with Stephon Marbury the summer after ninth grade. Marbury was a basketball player from New York City. He had found Kevin's phone number on a list at a basketball camp. He wanted to talk to Kevin because he thought that they were alike. They were the same age and both were becoming basketball stars. The two young men quickly became best friends without ever having met. They called each other often. Kevin even had to get a job at a fast-food restaurant to pay his phone bills.

High School Star

Kevin continued to work on improving his basketball skills. He attended a basketball camp the summer before 10th grade. He was among the best players at the camp. He averaged 18 points per game.

A HERO'S HERO

Magic Johnson

Kevin admired many basketball players as he grew up. One of his biggest basketball heroes was Laker guard Ervin "Magic" Johnson.

Johnson played point guard despite standing 6 feet, 9 inches (206 centimeters) tall. Most NBA point guards are much shorter than this. Few players of Johnson's height have the skills and quickness to play the position. Kevin admired this. Like Johnson, Kevin has abilities that few tall players have.

Johnson led the Michigan State Spartans team to an NCAA basketball championship in 1979. Later that year, he began his NBA career with the Lakers. Johnson went on to lead the Lakers to five NBA championships. He won the NBA's MVP award twice. He also helped Team USA win a gold medal in the 1992 Olympics.

Kevin went on to star for Mauldin the following season. He became the team's leader. College recruiters throughout the United States began to notice his size and skills.

Kevin was one of the biggest stars in high school basketball by 11th grade. He was 6 feet, 9 inches (206 centimeters) tall. Many college recruiters said that he was the top high school prospect in the United States. That year, Kevin averaged 21 points and 17 rebounds per game. The people of Mauldin filled the school's gym to watch him play.

Kevin led Mauldin to the 1994 South Carolina Class AAAA tournament. He scored 37 points in Mauldin's semifinal game. He also had 24 rebounds and six blocked shots. Mauldin won the game 60-55 to advance to the finals. But Mauldin lost the championship game 70-58. After the season, Kevin was named a first-team All-American.

CHAPTER 3

A Big Jump

Kevin attended Nike's all-star summer basketball camp after 11th grade. William Nelson was one of the camp's coaches. Nelson was amazed at Kevin's skills. He thought that Kevin could play any position on the court. Kevin could handle the ball and pass like a point guard. His rebounding skills were like those of a power forward. He shot three-pointers like a small forward. Kevin also was tall enough to play center.

Moving to Chicago
Nelson also was the basketball coach at Farragut Academy. This high school is in

Kevin attended Farragut Academy during his final year of high school.

Chicago, Illinois. Kevin's mother wanted to move the family. She thought that Kevin was receiving too much attention in South Carolina. Nelson convinced Kevin's mother to move the family to Chicago. Kevin would attend Farragut Academy.

The family moved to Chicago before Kevin's last year of high school. The move was difficult for the family. They lived in a small apartment on Chicago's west side. This is a poor area of the city. Kevin's mother worked two jobs to support the family.

The move to Chicago was good for Kevin's basketball career. He learned to play more aggressively on the court. He played against stronger competition. He also had more skilled teammates.

Kevin averaged 25 points and 18 rebounds per game that season. He led his team to the 1995 Illinois Class AA tournament. But the team lost in the semifinals. After the season, Kevin was named Mr. Basketball of Illinois. This award goes to the state's best high school

Kevin was named Mr. Basketball of Illinois during his final year of high school.

player. *USA Today* also named Kevin its National Player of the Year.

A Big Decision

Kevin wanted to go to college. After college, he hoped to play in the NBA. But Kevin had to take an entrance exam to get into college. Athletes must get a certain score on this test to participate in sports. Kevin did not score high enough on the test the first time he took it. He could not get a college scholarship unless he improved his score. He did not have enough money to attend college without a scholarship. Kevin took the test again.

Kevin's test scores did not come back right away. He waited several weeks for the results. He thought about going straight to the NBA. Kevin had to declare himself eligible for the 1995 NBA draft to do this. But the deadline for declaring was approaching. Kevin could not wait any longer for his test scores. He declared himself eligible for the draft three days before the deadline. Only four players born in North America had ever gone to the NBA without playing college basketball.

The NBA Draft

Many teams were unsure of Kevin's abilities before the draft. Kevin attended workouts for NBA teams. At one workout, he caught the attention of Kevin McHale. McHale is a former NBA star. He was a vice president for the Minnesota Timberwolves. McHale and

Flip Saunders of the Timberwolves was impressed with Kevin's skills.

Timberwolves' general manager Flip Saunders were amazed by Kevin's abilities. They knew after they left the workout that they were going to draft Kevin.

The 1995 NBA draft took place on June 28 at the SkyDome in Toronto, Canada. The Timberwolves selected Kevin with the fifth pick in the first round. Kevin's dream had come true. He was going to play in the NBA.

Chapter 4

The NBA

After the draft, Kevin signed a three-year, $5.6 million contract with the Timberwolves. He immediately started to prepare for the NBA. Kevin left for the Timberwolves' training camp in Minnesota. He worked hard during training camp. He knew that he had much to learn. He had to prove himself to his coaches and teammates. Many people did not believe a player who had just finished high school could be ready for the NBA.

On October 14, 1995, the Timberwolves played an exhibition game against the Milwaukee Bucks. Kevin put a rubber band

Kevin joined the Timberwolves in 1995.

around his ankle. He then stepped onto the court to play in his first professional basketball game.

Rookie Season

Kevin's first regular-season game was on November 3, 1995, against the Sacramento Kings. He entered the game with about 6 minutes remaining in the first quarter. Two minutes later, he scored his first points on a bank shot. Kevin took only four shots in the game. He made all four. But the Kings won the game 105-96.

Kevin did not play often during November. The Timberwolves lost most of their games during this time. In December, the team fired head coach Bill Blair. Saunders became the new head coach. Saunders wanted to help Kevin improve his skills. He gave Kevin more playing time. Kevin entered the starting lineup by mid-season. He averaged 14 points per game during the season's second half. He was named to the NBA's All-Rookie second team after the season ended.

Kevin quickly became one of the NBA's best defensive players.

Professional Success

In 1996, Kevin's friend Stephon Marbury decided to enter the NBA draft after one year of college. The Timberwolves made a trade to get him. Kevin and Stephon had always wanted to play on the same NBA team. They were determined to help make the Timberwolves into a winning team.

The Timberwolves began the 1996–97 season well. Forward Tom Gugliotta was named to the NBA Western Conference All-Star team at mid-season. No Timberwolves' player had ever been named to the team. Many fans hoped Kevin would be named to the team as well. But his name was not included when the list of players was released.

Before the All-Star break, Lakers' center Shaquille O'Neal suffered an injury. He could not play in the All-Star Game. The team's coaches selected Kevin to take O'Neal's place. Kevin and Gugliotta became the first Timberwolves' All-Stars.

The Timberwolves finished the season with a 40-42 record. This record earned them a spot in the playoffs. The Timberwolves faced the Houston Rockets in the first round. The Rockets easily swept the Timberwolves 3-0. Kevin averaged 17.3 points per game in the series.

Kevin had one year left on his contract after the 1996–97 season. The Timberwolves were worried about letting him become a free agent

Kevin's friend Stephon Marbury joined the Timberwolves in 1996.

after the season. They wanted to make sure no other team could sign Kevin. On October 1, 1997, the Timberwolves and Kevin agreed to a six-year contract extension. The contract would pay Kevin a total of $126 million.

High Hopes

The Timberwolves entered the 1997–98 season with high hopes. All three of the team's stars were returning. It was Kevin's third season. Many expected him to become one of the best forwards in the game.

Kevin recorded his first triple-double on January 3, 1998, against the Denver Nuggets. He had 18 points, 13 rebounds, and 10 assists. This showed the rest of the league that he could do more than just score.

In February, NBA fans voted Kevin onto the Western Conference All-Star team. He was a starting forward in the game. At 21, he also was the second youngest player ever to start in an All-Star Game.

The Timberwolves ended the season with a 45-37 record. It was the team's first winning

Kevin averaged 18.5 points and 9.6 rebounds per game during the 1997–98 season.

season. They earned the seventh playoff spot in the Western Conference. They played the Seattle Supersonics in the first round of the playoffs. No one expected the Timberwolves to keep the series close. Gugliotta had suffered an injury during the season. He could not play in the playoffs. This meant Kevin would receive most of Seattle's defensive attention.

The Timberwolves faced the Spurs in the 1999 playoffs.

The Playoffs
The first two games of the series were in Seattle. Kevin scored 18 points and had 18 rebounds in the first game. But the Supersonics won 108-83.

The Timberwolves played much better in the second game. Marbury led the team with 25 points. Kevin scored 15. The Timberwolves won their first playoff game 98-93. The series was tied 1-1.

The next two games were in Minnesota. In the third game, the Timberwolves were behind by five points after three quarters. But Kevin and his teammates began the fourth quarter by outscoring Seattle 18-4. Kevin finished this run with a hard slam dunk. He then took over the game. He scored seven points in the final five minutes and nine seconds of play. The Timberwolves won 98-90. They led the series 2-1. One more win would advance them to the second round.

The Timberwolves did not win another game. In the fourth game, Kevin scored 20 points and had 10 rebounds. But that was not enough. Seattle won the game 92-88. The Supersonics also won the fifth game in Seattle 97-84. The Timberwolves' season was over.

A Shortened Season

NBA owners were concerned about Kevin's huge contract. The owners feared that many of the other players also would demand huge salaries. They realized that they needed a new agreement with the players. They wanted a limit on players' salaries. The players did not want a limit on their salaries. The two sides could not come to an agreement before the 1998–99 season. The owners then locked out the players. This meant the owners would not start the season until the two sides reached an agreement. The owners would not pay the players during this time.

In early 1999, the owners and the players finally agreed to set limits on player salaries. But much of the season had been lost to the lockout. The teams agreed to shorten the season.

The Timberwolves went through many changes during this time. Gugliotta left the team as a free agent. Marbury was unhappy in Minnesota. He demanded to be traded. Soon, Kevin was the only star on the team.

Kevin led the Timberwolves to a 25-25 record. This gave them the final playoff spot in the Western Conference. They faced the powerful San Antonio Spurs in the first round. The Spurs won the first game 99-86. The Timberwolves won the second game 80-71. But they lost the next two games. The team was once again out of the playoffs.

The Timberwolves defeated the Spurs 80-71 in the second game of their 1999 playoff series.

CHAPTER 5

Kevin Garnett Today

Many basketball fans and experts consider Kevin the best forward in the game today. Some believe he is the best all-around player in the NBA. Kevin enjoys his success. But he wants more. He wants to win a championship with the Timberwolves.

Kevin attends college classes during the off-season. He believes that education is important. He also knows that he is a role model for many children. He wants to show them that everyone needs an education.

Many basketball experts believe Kevin is the best all-around player in the NBA.

Kevin finished second in the 1999–2000 MVP voting.

The 1999–2000 Season

Kevin continued to improve in 1999–2000. He averaged 22.9 points and 11.8 rebounds per game. He was named as a starter for the All-Star Game. He scored 24 points in the game. He also had 10 rebounds and blocked six shots.

Kevin also earned honors after the season. He was named to the All-NBA team and the

All-NBA defensive team. He finished second to Shaquille O'Neal in the MVP voting.

The Timberwolves faced the Portland Trailblazers in the first round of the playoffs. Portland had the second best record in the NBA during the regular season. Portland won the first two games of the series 91-88 and 86-82. Minnesota won the third game 94-87. But it was not enough. Portland won the fourth game 85-77. The Timberwolves had lost the first round of the playoffs again.

Loss of a Friend

On May 20, 2000, Timberwolves' guard Malik Sealy was killed in a car accident near Minneapolis, Minnesota. Sealy was returning home late at night from Kevin's birthday party.

Sealy's death was difficult for Kevin. Sealy was one of his best friends on the team. During high school, Kevin had admired Sealy. Kevin even chose to wear number 21 when he entered the NBA because that had been Sealy's number.

Giving Back

Kevin has not forgotten his hometown and the children who live there. He lives in Minnesota now. But he often makes trips to Mauldin to visit his friends and fans. He sometimes plays basketball with his friends at Springfield Park. He even paid to have the basketball court there resurfaced. This was his gift to the children of Mauldin. In 1996, Mauldin gave Kevin the key to the city. This is an honor towns and cities sometimes give famous residents.

Kevin also helps children in Minnesota. He makes many visits to children's hospitals. He talks to sick children. He signs autographs and tries to help them forget about their illnesses. Kevin also gives money to help pay the medical expenses of children whose parents cannot afford it.

Most experts believe that Kevin will be among the NBA's best players for years to come.

Career Highlights

1976—Kevin is born in Greenville, South Carolina, on May 19.

1991–1992—Kevin plays for Mauldin High School's basketball team as a ninth grader.

1994—Kevin leads Mauldin to the 1994 South Carolina Class AAAA tournament; he is named a first-team All-American; he moves with his family to Chicago, Illinois, to attend Farragut Academy.

1995—Kevin leads Farragut to the semifinals of the Illinois Class AA tournament; he is named Mr. Basketball of Illinois; he declares himself eligible for the 1995 NBA draft and is drafted by the Minnesota Timberwolves; Kevin plays in his first NBA game on November 3.

1996—Kevin is named to the NBA's All-Rookie second team.

1997—Kevin plays in his first NBA All-Star Game; he signs a $126 million contract extension with the Timberwolves.

1998—Kevin records his first triple-double; fans vote him as a starter for the NBA All-Star Game.

1999—Kevin leads Team USA to the championship in the Olympic Qualifying Tournament.

2000—Kevin is named to the All-NBA team and the All-NBA Defensive Team; he helps Team USA wins the Olympic gold medal.

Words to Know

contract (KON-trakt)—an agreement between an owner and a player; contracts determine players' salaries.

endorse (en-DORSS)—to sponsor a product by appearing in advertisements

free agent (FREE AY-juhnt)—a player who is free to sign with any team

lockout (LOK-out)—a period of time in which owners prevent players from reporting to their teams; owners do not pay players during a lockout.

rookie (RUK-ee)—a first-year player

scholarship (SKOL-ur-ship)—a grant of money that helps a student pay for college

To Learn More

Deegan, Paul. *Kevin Garnett.* Basketball Legends. Philadelphia: Chelsea House Publishers, 1999.

Dougherty, Terri. *Kevin Garnett.* Jam Session. Edina, Minn.: Abdo, 1999.

Macnow, Glen. *Sports Great Kevin Garnett.* Sports Great Books. Berkeley Heights, N.J.: Enslow Publishers, 2000.

Torres, John Albert. *Kevin Garnett: "Da Kid."* Minneapolis: Lerner, 2000.

Useful Addresses

The Basketball Hall of Fame
P.O. Box 179
1150 West Columbus Avenue
Springfield, MA 01101-0179

Kevin Garnett
c/o Minnesota Timberwolves
Target Center
600 First Avenue North
Minneapolis, MN 55401

Internet Sites

CBS Sportsline.com—Kevin Garnett
http://cbs.sportsline.com/u/basketball/nba/
    players/6581.htm

ESPN.com—NBA
http://sports.espn.go.com/nba/index

NBA.com
http://www.nba.com

USA Basketball—Kevin Garnett
http://www.usabasketball.com/Men/
    garnett_bio.html

Index

All-American, 17
All-NBA defensive team, 8, 39
All-NBA team, 8, 38
All-Star Game, 29, 30, 38

Blair, Bill, 26

Farragut Academy, 19, 20
Fisher, James, 13

Garnett, Shirley, 11, 12
Greenville, South Carolina, 11
Gugliotta, Tom, 29, 31, 34

Irby, Ernest, 11, 12

lockout, 34

Marbury, Stephon, 15, 27, 32, 34
Mauldin, South Carolina, 11, 17, 40

McCullough, O'Lewis, 11
McHale, Kevin, 22
Most Valuable Player (MVP), 8, 39
Mr. Basketball of Illinois, 20

Nelson, William, 19–20
Nike, 8, 19

Olympic Qualifying Tournament, 5
O'Neal, Shaquille, 8, 29, 39

Payton, Gary, 6

San Juan, Puerto Rico, 5
Saunders, Flip, 23, 26
Sealy, Malik, 39–40
Springfield Park, 12, 40

Team USA, 5–6, 8
triple-double, 30